# Canada's Natural Wonders

**Joanne Richter**

## Scholastic Canada Ltd.

Toronto  New York  London  Auckland  Sydney
Mexico City  New Delhi  Hong Kong  Buenos Aires

**Photo Credits**
Cover (upper left): Firstlight/ Mike Grandmaison
Cover (upper right, lower right, lower left), pp. iv, 30, 50, 55: Firstlight
Back cover: Northern Saskatchewan Archives, Pahkisimon Nuye?áh Library System
La Ronge, Saskatchewan
pp. 2, 3, 5, 6, 11, 17, 20, 21, 26, 34, 38, 39, 51, 52, 53, 56, 57, 61, 62, 63: istock
pp. 8–10, 12, 18, 19: Natural Resources Canada images produced with permission
of Natural Resources Canada. Her Majesty the Queen in Right of Canada.
p. 13: Notman Studio / Library and Archives Canada / C-007606
p. 14: Paul Nopper
p. 15: Jacques Descloitres, MODIS Land Rapid Response Team, NASA/GSFC
p. 23: Jamie Jennings
p. 25: Ron Erwin Photography
pp. 27 and 31: Photo courtesy of Becky Cook
p. 29: David Callan
p. 32: Image courtesy of the Image Science & Analysis Laboratory, NASA Johnson
Space Center; Mission: ISS006 Roll: E Frame: 28775
p. 33: Image courtesy NASA/GSFC/LaRC/JPL, MISR Team
p. 37: Hydro-Québec
p. 41: Niagara Falls (Ontario) Public Library
p. 42: Image courtesy of the Image Science & Analysis Laboratory, NASA Johnson
Space Center; Mission: ISS005 Roll: E Frame: 5646
p. 44: ENVIRO FOTO
p. 45: Photo courtesy of Saskatchewan Environment
p. 46: ENVIRO FOTO
p. 48: ENVIRO FOTO
p. 59: Photo courtesy The Burgess Shale Foundation

Many thanks to Godfrey Nowlan of the Geological Survey of Canada for his assistance in
reviewing this book.

**Library and Archives Canada Cataloguing in Publication**
Richter, Joanne
    Canada's natural wonders / Joanne Richter.

(Canada close up)
ISBN 978-0-545-99780-5

    1. Natural monuments—Canada—Juvenile literature.   2.  Physical
geography—Canada—Juvenile literature.   I. Title.   II. Series: Canada
close up (Markham, Ont.)

FC58.R52 2008              j917.102              C2007-904455-7

ISBN-10 0-545-99780-1

6  5  4  3  2              Printed in Canada              09  10  11  12

# Table of Contents

**Pronunciation Guide**

We've given you a guide on how to say some of the new words you will find in this book. The syllable that's in **bold** type is stressed, or said a little louder than the others. Here is a key to the vowel sounds in this book:

a as in at; **ay** as in day; ee as in see; o as in ocean; **oo** as in food; u as in but; i as in pit; **ah** as in pot; **ow** as in pout

# Introduction

What picture comes to mind when you think of Canada? Forest-covered mountains? Sparkling lakes and rivers? Flat prairies?

How about bone-dry deserts, ice fields and rainforests? Believe it or not, Canada has all of these and more.

Sometimes natural forces make unusual features that stand out from the areas around them. People enjoy visiting them and want to learn more about them. We call these features landmarks.

Let's take a tour of just a few of these wonderful places!

## Chapter 1

# Shaped by Nature

Have you ever wondered how mountains, lakes and waterfalls are made? Two powerful forces of nature play the biggest role.

The first force is the movement of Earth's **crust**. The crust is the rocky outside layer of our planet. It is under our oceans and makes up all of Earth's dry land. Scientists who study Earth's crust have found out that it is broken up into very large pieces called **plates**.

The plates are always moving, so the crust does a lot of pushing and pulling. Sometimes the edges of two plates are pushed together so hard that they have nowhere to go but up. Sometimes one plate slides on top of the other plate. A plate might even bend or fold.

The movement of Earth's plates caused mountains to rise.

No matter how a plate moves, what happens in the end is the same. Flat land is pushed up and then eroded. It forms mountains and valleys. Of course, all this takes a very long time. Many of Earth's plates move only two centimetres in a whole year. Mountains take millions of years to form.

Try this yourself: lay two pieces of paper side by side on a flat surface so their edges meet. Slowly push the pieces against each other. What happens?

🍁 Glaciers have also helped to form unique land features.

Canada's second-biggest land shapers are **glaciers**. A glacier is a flowing "river" of ice. Glaciers are formed in cold places, when snowflakes pack together into a solid mound of ice. Glaciers flow very slowly because their ice is heavy. Glaciers move so slowly that they seem to stand still. Most move only 100 to 200 metres each year. You might walk that distance in a minute or two.

When glaciers move, they pick up rock and stones that grind the rock beneath. They scrape deep bowl shapes and deep valleys into the land. When they melt, their waters flow into these low areas, creating lakes and rivers.

Canada's glaciers are found on the high mountaintops of the west and in the Arctic. But during the last **ice age**, which ended about 10,000 years ago, most of Canada was covered with glacier ice.

Moving plates and glacier ice have created many unique Canadian landmarks, but other forces have played a part, too. Let's find out more!

## Chapter 2

# Mount Logan

If you visit Kluane [kloo-**ah**-nee] National Park in the Yukon Territory, you'll come face to face with a family of giants. They're the Saint Elias Mountains and they tower over Canada. The highest peak, Mount Logan, is 5,959 metres tall. That's higher than 10 CN Towers stacked on top of one another!

Canada's tallest mountain is also the second-tallest in North America. But scientists believe that it's actually the biggest mountain in the whole world. That's because its base measures more than 100 kilometres around.

Mount Logan is still growing. The Saint Elias Mountains were formed over millions of years by the pushing together and sliding of two of Earth's plates. One of the plates is still slowly pushing Mount Logan higher.

The Saint Elias mountains took millions of years to form.

The cracks that separate plates are called **fault lines**. When fault lines are active, earthquakes can happen! A very old fault line runs right through Mount Logan. Luckily, it has been inactive for about 50 million years.

Because Mount Logan is so tall and covered in ice, it's an unfriendly place for most animals. But you might find lynx, cougars, grizzly bears, Dall's sheep or wolverines around the mountain. They may even stray onto the mountain from time to time.

Lynx are found around the mountain.

Wolverines may wander onto Mount Logan.

Mount Logan is a tough place for people to survive, too. It's very cold near the **summit**, or top, of the mountain. Avalanches happen often. Still, people come from all over the world to climb it. The first climbers to make it to the top were a team of Canadians and Americans in 1925. Since then, hundreds more have reached the summit. Sadly, at least 11 people have died trying.

🍁 Each year people climb Mount Logan.

In 1842, a gifted scientist named Sir William Logan founded the Geological Survey of Canada for the study of earth science. He did such important work that Mount Logan was named in his honour many years later. He would surely be proud to share his name with such a majestic mountain.

Sir William Logan

## Chapter 3

# Baffin Island Ice Caps

In Inuktitut, the language of the Inuit, the name for an ice cap is auyuittuq [ow-**you**-ee-tuk] — "land that never melts." But on Baffin Island in Nunavut, the ice caps are melting. This has some scientists worried.

Ice caps, dome-shaped glaciers of smooth ice, are found across the eastern Canadian Arctic. They are part of a group of very old glaciers that have survived from the last ice age.

Two large ice caps are found on Baffin Island, the fifth-largest island in the world. The Barnes Ice Cap lies almost right in the middle of the island. The Penny Ice Cap sits like a crown on top of the high mountains of Auyuittuq National Park.

The oldest ice of the Barnes Ice Cap is believed to be 100,000 years old. Its thickest parts measure 550 metres from top to bottom.
That's taller than the CN Tower!

There are few plants or animals living near the Penny Ice Cap, since it's so high up. But the Barnes Ice Cap is an important part of everyday life for both the Inuit people and the animals of Baffin Island. Even on warm summer days, a cool breeze blows down from the ice cap. Herds of caribou spend much of the spring and summer near the ice. Both caribou and people travel across it to get from place to place. Melting ice from the cap flows in swift rivers and creates wetlands where snow geese come to nest.

🍁 Caribou use the ice caps to travel from one place to another.

🍁 Scientists study the ice caps to learn more about weather patterns.

The world's ice caps and glaciers provide a lot of Earth's fresh water. But scientists say the ice caps and glaciers are getting smaller. They are melting faster than new snow can build them up. Canada's ice caps, such as the Barnes and Penny, are melting the fastest. What is happening to the Baffin Island ice caps helps scientists understand weather patterns today and predict what will come tomorrow.

Ice caps can tell us about the past, too. Land around the edges of the shrinking caps is being uncovered for the first time in 10,000 years. People are excited to study this land. It might provide important clues about how and why the last ice age ended. Even the ice itself is like a time capsule from long ago. Air bubbles trapped inside the ice can tell scientists what the weather was like thousands of years ago!

When the ice caps melt, they reveal land that has long been covered.

## Chapter 4

# Gros Morne National Park

Its name means "Big Gloomy" in French, but Gros Morne [gros morn] National Park is sure to put you in a good mood. That's because it is one of the most beautiful parks in the world.

Gros Morne is part of the Appalachian Mountains, which stretch from Newfoundland all the way down to the southern United States. These mountains were created about 400 million years ago, when two of Earth's plates smashed into each other. But the rock itself is actually 1.2 billion years old!

Since then, the land at Gros Morne has been shaped over and over again. Moving plates, glaciers, wind and the ocean have all played a part. Scientists have found so many interesting details in the rocks there, it's almost as though Gros Morne is telling its own story!

Gros Morne has a whole collection of beautiful features. You can find beaches, waterfalls and amazing rock formations there. One of the highlights of the park is Western Brook Pond. But it's no ordinary pond. Western Brook Pond is a 10,000-year-old **fjord** [feeyord] lake.

Western Brook Pond is just one of the stunning features of Gros Morne National Park.

During the last ice age, a glacier scraped its way through the rock on its way to the ocean. It left behind a long, narrow ocean **inlet** surrounded by two tall, steep mountain cliffs. Over time the mouth of the fjord closed off from the ocean. The fjord filled with fresh water instead.

The most unusual feature at the park is known as the Tablelands. If you went for a walk there, you might think you were on Mars.

The yellowish-tan rock of the Tablelands is called peridotite [pe-*rid*-o-tite]. It is made up of minerals that most plants can't grow in. The rest of Gros Morne, though, is home to many different plants and animals. You might see caribou, lynx or even an Arctic hare roaming the land.

The Tablelands look very much like a desert, but instead of sand, the ground is rock from Earth's **mantle**. Normally, this rock is only found deep underground. But when two plates collided, some mantle rock was pushed up from beneath the ocean. Over time, the layer above it **eroded**, or wore away. This uncovered the mantle rock.

In 1973 Canada made the Gros Morne area a national park. Now its unique features are being preserved, and people from all over Canada can discover the story of the rocks for themselves.

🍁 The Tablelands might remind you of Mars.

## Chapter 5

# Bay of Fundy

Twice every day, like clockwork, the world's highest ocean tides come rushing into the Bay of Fundy. The bay stretches between New Brunswick and Nova Scotia, and is 270 kilometres long. A car might drive this distance in two and a half hours on a highway.

The Bay of Fundy began its life more than 200 million years ago. When two of Earth's plates pulled apart, the crack, or rift, in between became a valley. Glaciers scraped out the valley even more until finally the ocean came rushing in.

Have you ever made waves in a bathtub? You have to push on the water with a steady rhythm to get the waves really rolling. That's what happens in the Bay of Fundy. The source of the rhythm is the pull of **gravity** between Earth and the Moon. There are two spots in the Earth's spin where this pull is strongest, and the Bay of Fundy passes both of them every day.

All oceans have high and low tides. The Bay of Fundy tides are so high because of the bay's shape. At high tide, water is forced into a tight space. It has nowhere to go but up onto the surrounding shores.

The tides in the Bay of Fundy can sometimes rise and fall as high as a four-storey building! In just 12 hours, 100 billion tons of ocean water flows into the bay and then back out to the ocean. That's enough water to fill 100 bathtubs for every person on Earth!

🍁 There's a big difference between high tide and low tide.

This powerful rush of water has carved interesting shapes into the cliffs along the shore. At New Brunswick's Hopewell Rocks, flowerpot-shaped pillars of rock stick out from the ocean.

Hopewell Rocks have many interesting rock shapes.

The Bay of Fundy's tides stir up water and **sediment** from the very bottom of the ocean. This makes the water ice-cold and very muddy-looking. But this water is full of nutrients. When it reaches shallow areas, it's the perfect place for tiny animals called plankton to grow.

Waters full of plankton are a banquet for whales! The Bay of Fundy is a feeding ground for about 15 whale species,

Whale watching in the Bay of Fundy can be very exciting.

including the humpback and the endangered right whale. Dolphins and sharks swim the waters, too. Birds such as sandpipers feast on tiny creatures that live on the muddy shore.

Many tourists visit the bay every summer. There is nothing quite like taking a stroll along the ocean floor at low tide, only to see it covered in deep water just six hours later!

## Chapter 6

# Manicouagan Crater

In the forests of Northern Quebec, a ring-shaped lake surrounds a perfectly round island. These are the first hints to a landmark that's really out of this world.

The Manicouagan [ma-ni-coo-**ah**-gan] Crater is known as the "eye of Quebec." It's one of the oldest and largest **meteorite impact craters** in the world.

A meteorite impact crater is formed when a chunk of rock from space falls to Earth. The rock has a lot of energy. Most of the time, it explodes before it hits the ground. When it hits Earth, it makes a large hole. If the impact is big enough it may even bring up rock from deep below the Earth's surface. People have discovered only about 170 impact craters on Earth. There should be more, but many have been eroded by glaciers and other natural forces.

🍁 Large meteorites hitting Earth have created many impact craters around the world.

The Manicouagan Crater didn't wear away because the meteorite landed in the very hard rock known as the **Canadian Shield.** Glaciers did sweep away the rim of the crater. They also dug a deep trench, in a ring shape, where the rock was broken up by the shock of the crash.

If you want to see why an impact site has a ring shape, try dropping a rock into sand. Do you see how shock waves travel through the sand from where the rock was dropped?

The Manicouagan Crater was formed about 214 million years ago. Imagine a space rock the size of a small town hurtling to Earth at a speed of up to 60 kilometres per second. That's faster than today's space shuttles can travel!

The crash was so powerful that the centre of the crater turned to liquid. It became a deep pool of melted rock that may have taken thousands of years to cool. The impact probably set off earthquakes and threw giant fireballs for very long distances.

Scientists believe that the dinosaurs became extinct because of another, larger meteorite crash. Many animal species died out around the same time as the Manicouagan impact. Some people thought they might have died because of this meteorite. But tests have shown that this was not true.

Today, the crater is a peaceful place. The deep outside ring is filled with water, which is used to generate electricity. The land inside the ring has become an island, where ancient forests still grow. Moose live on the island year-round, and feed at the water's edge. Many people would like to see the whole island protected as a national park.

🍁 The Daniel Johnson Dam uses the water from Manicouagan Crater to provide us with electricity.

## Chapter 7

# Niagara Falls

One of Canada's most famous places to sightsee is more than just a pretty view. It was shaped after years of hard work by forces deep inside Earth, as well as glaciers. And it's an amazing example of the power of water!

Niagara Falls is actually three falls. The mighty Niagara River flows over all three at the border between Ontario and the United States. But nearly all of the water rushes over Horseshoe Falls, on the Canadian side. Horseshoe Falls was named for its horseshoe shape.

The force of Horseshoe Falls is so strong that it can never completely freeze in winter. But in 1848, an ice jam above the falls caused it to run nearly dry for two days. People gathered to see the strange sight. Some walked on the river bed. Some people even found items that had been lost under water for hundreds of years.

Horseshoe Falls is not the world's tallest waterfall. But it's one of the most exciting to see because so much water thunders over it. When the flow is strongest, enough water to fill more than 400 swimming pools tumbles over the falls each minute!

Can you imagine walking through Niagara Falls without getting wet?

The Falls wouldn't have happened without the Niagara Escarpment. This tall ridge of tilted rock was once at the bottom of an ancient ocean that covered most of Ontario. The limestone rock of the escarpment is rich in fossils.

After the last ice age, glaciers left behind the beginnings of North America's Great Lakes. Water from Lake Erie began to drain toward Lake Ontario, which is lower. The route it took became the Niagara River. The river flowed right over the Niagara Escarpment, and the falls were born.

This satellite image taken from space shows the Niagara River running into Lake Ontario. The Falls are in the centre.

At first, the falls were pretty tiny. The river fell only 11 metres. That's about as tall as the average maple tree. Today, the drop from Horseshoe Falls is nearly five times as high. This is because the river wears away the rock below. As this happens, the falls move farther up the river. The falls are now 11 kilometres away from where they first began.

The first people to live by the falls were the Ongiara, an Iroquois tribe. For them, Horseshoe Falls was the kingdom of the Thunder God. A lot of animals make their home by the falls, too. The river is an important **habitat** for birds such as the bald eagle and peregrine falcon, and fish like lake sturgeon and salmon. Yes, fish do go over the falls!

## Chapter 8

# Athabasca Sand Dunes

Imagine flying over the forests of northern Saskatchewan. In the distance, you can see a large lake. Beside it, spreading for kilometres, is . . . a white sand desert?

It's sand all right, but the Athabasca Sand Dunes are not a part of a desert. There's plenty of water and wildlife here.

According to a legend of the Dene [**deh**-neh] First Nation, a giant beaver battered the earth with his tail and turned it into sand. Scientists say that the dunes, or sand hills, were created when glaciers from the last ice age melted away. They left tons of sand behind at the bottom of Lake Athabasca. When the lake shrank, the sand was uncovered.

The sand dunes can be breathtaking.

Today, the Athabasca Sand Dunes are part of the largest active dune system in the world. The hills and ridges are always being pushed and pulled into new shapes by wind and water. The dunes stretch for 100 kilometres along Lake Athabasca, the largest lake in Saskatchewan. The tallest dunes reach as high as an eight-storey building.

The wind and blowing sands make interesting sculptures from the small rocks in the dunes, too. They polish them until they're smooth and flat. These wind-shaped rocks are called **ventifacts**. In some areas, small polished rocks are tightly packed together over a large area. They're almost like an old-fashioned cobblestone road. These areas are known as desert pavement.

Sometimes the wind sweeps the sand right over a group of trees. Without air, light or water, the trees die. Years later, the sand blows somewhere new, uncovering what looks like a skeleton forest.

Some areas of the dunes don't move, though. This is where plants can grow. Ten species of plants grow in the Athabasca Sand Dunes that aren't found anywhere else in the world. The dunes are also home to wild orchids and animals such as wolves, caribou, eagles and Arctic terns.

🍁 There are many beautiful and unique plants found throughout the dunes.

The Dene people have long fished and hunted at Lake Athabasca. Visitors are welcome to come and explore the Athabasca Sand Dunes, too. But this provincial park is deep in the wilderness. You'll need to arrive by float plane!

## Chapter 9

# Alberta Badlands

Seventy-five million years ago, Alberta's badlands area was a lush, swampy forest full of dinosaurs. When a dinosaur died, its body often stayed trapped in the wetland mud. Over time, the mud hardened into rock.

Long after the dinosaurs disappeared, the glaciers of the last ice age carved the soft rock into unusual shapes. The rushing waters from the melting ice shaped the rock, too. The soil attached to the rock was eroded away by ice, wind and water. Today, Alberta's badlands are a true desert, filled with amazing rock sculptures.

Have you ever heard of a hoodoo? These famous badlands shapes look like mushrooms. The top layers of hard rock have worn away more slowly than the lower layers of soft sandstone.

Hoodoos are found throughout the Badlands.

Tall canyon cliffs and dry riverbeds called **coulees** are also found in the badlands landscape.

Best of all, the badlands are a dinosaur hunter's dream! Because so much rock has worn away, dinosaur bones are there for anyone to find. The first dinosaur discovery was in 1884, when Joseph Tyrrell found an Albertosaurus skull.

Today, the Royal Tyrrell Museum is a highlight of the badlands. Among its treasures are fossils of all sorts, including many dinosaur skeletons.

A *Tyrannosaurus rex* skeleton

This dry, hilly landscape is called the badlands because it is difficult to travel through on foot or horseback.

The Blackfoot and Cree people travelled and hunted bison through the badlands for thousands of years. Settlers from Europe first came to the area just over a hundred years ago to mine coal found in the rock. They used it as fuel for heating and cooking. At one time, there were 139 coal mines in the area. These all closed down after better fuels became available. Now, empty towns have been left behind where the miners once lived. These are known as "ghost towns."

There's still plenty of life in the badlands. The plants and animals that thrive there that are specially adapted to living in a desert. Bison still roam the plains, as do mule deer. Plants like cactus, greasewood and sage need little water to survive here.

Today, Alberta's badlands continue to wear away. Every year, four millimetres of rock is lost to the wind and rivers. That may not sound like much, but it means that new dinosaur finds are always just around the corner.

🍁 Bison roam the badlands.

## Chapter 10

# Canadian Rockies

The Canadian Rockies began to form 75 million years ago. That's very young for mountains. But some of the rock they're made of is actually 800 million years old!

The Rocky Mountains are part
of a large mountain system that
stretches from Alaska through
western Canada down into the
United States. The part of the
system in Canada is known as
the Canadian Rockies.

The land where the Rockies now
stand was once flat. Then one of
Earth's plates beneath the Pacific
Ocean began to push very hard
against the plate beneath western
Canada. This made its soft rock fold
and fracture. A big bulge started to
form in western Canada. The rock
was pushed high up. The pushing
continued, and the rocks were
pushed farther and farther inland,
away from the ocean, and higher
and higher. Over a long time, the
wearing away of the bulge began to
reveal the jagged mountains.

The rock of the ancient ocean floor was pushed up very high. Now, as the soft rock erodes, people sometimes discover seashells on mountain peaks! An important fossil bed called the Burgess Shale has also been discovered there. The fossils tell scientists a lot about prehistoric underwater life. They are so well-preserved that scientists can even study the food the animals ate!

🍁 The Burgess Shale can tell scientists a lot about prehistoric life.

Ice age glaciers carved deep bowl-shaped valleys between the jagged mountains of the Canadian Rockies. They also left behind **moraines**, large piles of rocks that were picked up by a flowing glacier and dropped in one spot when the glacier melted.

Glaciers still flow down many valleys of the Canadian Rockies. The Columbia Icefield is the biggest glacier left in Alberta's Rockies. Apart from those found in the Arctic, it's the largest ice cap in the world. The water that melts away from it feeds three different oceans!

Many lakes in the Canadian Rockies are filled with water from melted glacier ice. This water holds fine particles. When sunlight hits the water, the particles reflect only blue light. This makes the water a surprising milky blue.

🍁 The milky blue colour of the lakes in the Rockies is caused by tiny particles.

The steep mountainsides of the Rockies are perfect for many wild animals, such as grizzly bears, bighorn sheep and mountain goats. Eagles soar high over forests of lodgepole pine, spruce and fir. Elk browse for food in the green valleys.

🍁 Grizzly bears are common in the Rockies.

Many people visit the Rockies for some outdoor fun.

The Rockies are not Canada's highest mountains, but they are world-famous for their beautiful scenery. And they're the perfect place for backpacking, rock climbing and skiing.

Canada's landscapes are always changing. Earth's plates keep moving, and wind, water and ice continue to erode the rocks. What do you think our landmarks will look like in a hundred years? A thousand years? A million?

# Glossary

**Canadian Shield:** an area of very hard, ancient rock that lies beneath most of central and eastern Canada

**coulees:** valleys created by streams of water when glaciers melt

**crust:** the hard, rocky covering of Earth

**eroded:** when something has been gradually worn away

**glaciers:** slow-moving masses of ice

**gravity:** the force that pulls smaller objects toward larger objects; gravity pulls things toward Earth

**habitat:** the place in nature where a plant or animal usually lives

**ice age:** a time in Earth's history when glaciers covered large areas of land most of the time

**inlet:** a narrow opening in the land where the ocean meets the shore

**mantle:** a thick layer of rock in the earth that is beneath the **crust**

**meteorite impact craters:** large holes in the ground made when meteorites hit Earth

**moraines:** soil and rock that were carried by glaciers and then dropped as the glaciers melted

**plates:** large pieces of the Earth's **crust** that are in constant motion

**sediment:** material that settles to the bottom of a liquid

**summit:** the top

**ventifacts:** stones that are shaped and smoothed by the wind